The New Baby

Written by Mary Packard

Illustrated by Amanda Haley

My First
READER

children's press®

A Division of Scholastic Inc.
New York Toronto London Auckland Sydney
Mexico City New Delhi Hong Kong
Danbury, Connecticut

Library of Congress Cataloging-in-Publication Data

Packard, Mary.
  The new baby / written by Mary Packard ; illustrated by Amanda Haley.
      p. cm. – (My first reader)
Summary: A boy is a little jealous of his new baby brother until mommy
gives him a hug and the new baby gives him a smile.
  ISBN 0-516-24409-4 (lib. bdg.)   0-516-25506-1 (pbk.)
  [1. Babies–Fiction. 2. Sibling rivalry–Fiction. 3. Stories in
rhyme.] I. Haley, Amanda, ill. II. Title. III. Series.
  PZ8.3.P125Ne 2004
  [E]–dc22
                                2003015918

Text © 2004 Nancy Hall, Inc.
Illustrations © 2004 Amanda Haley
All rights reserved.
Published in 2004 by Children's Press, an imprint of Scholastic Library Publishing.
Published simultaneously in Canada.
Printed in the United States of America.

1 2 3 4 5 6 7 8 9 10 R 13 12 11 10 09 08 07 06 05 04

Note to Parents and Teachers

Once a reader can recognize and identify the 48 words used to tell this story, he or she will be able to successfully read the entire book. These 48 words are repeated throughout the story, so that young readers will be able to recognize the words easily and understand their meaning.

The 48 words used in this book are:

a	come	home	noisy	to
and	crying	hug	one	today
at	daddy	I	says	too
baby	do	is	see	touch
boy	give	look	smiling	toy
brother	gives	love	squeak	what
busy	has	make	stay	with
came	he	me	stops	you
can	him	mommy	the	
cheek	his	my	think	

4

A baby came home
with Mommy today.

My daddy says he
has come home to stay.

Mommy is smiling
and gives him a toy.

9

I think the baby is one noisy boy.

"Look, Mommy, look, Mommy,
look at me, too!"

13

"Come give me a hug,"
Mommy says. "I love you."

15

Mommy is busy.

Daddy is, too.

The baby is crying.

What can I do?

I give him his toy.

I make his toy squeak.

The baby stops crying.

I touch his cheek.

"Look, Mommy, look, Daddy.
Come look and see."

"My baby brother is smiling at me!"

ABOUT THE AUTHOR

Mary Packard has been writing children's books for as long as she can remember. She lives in Northport, New York, with her family. Besides writing, she loves music, theater, animals, and, of course, children of all ages. Packard understands that when a new baby comes home, it seems like nothing will ever be the same again. She would like older siblings to know that the one thing that will always stay the same is their parents' love for them.

ABOUT THE ILLUSTRATOR

Amanda Haley has a BFA from the School of the Art Institute of Chicago. She has been a freelance illustrator for more than ten years, illustrating greeting cards, magazines, and more than thirty children's books. Haley lives and gardens in Cincinnati, Ohio, with her husband, Brian, and cherished dog, Sally.